I0224642

POCKET MANDALAS

Visual Meditations to Stress Less and Encourage Peace

Melissa Valdellon, O.D.

IMPORTANT MEDICAL DISCLAIMER: This book is intended as a reference volume only, not as a medical manual. The information given here is designed to help you make informed decisions about your health. It is not intended or implied to be a substitute for any treatment prescribed by, or medical advice given by, your doctor. All of the content, including text, images, and information contained in this book is for general purposes only. If you suspect that you have a medical problem or have any concerns whatsoever, please seek competent medical help immediately.

POCKET MANDALAS. Copyright © 2016 by Melissa Valdellon. All rights reserved. This book may not be reproduced in whole or in part, stored in a retrieval system, or transmitted in any form or by any means – electronic, mechanical, or other – without written permission from the copyright holder, except by a reviewer, who may quote brief passages in a review.

Published by Melissa Valdellon
www.melissavaldellon.com

Cover design by kelvintang of Fiverr
Cover image "Invitation" by Melissa Valdellon
Author photograph by Jennifer Michelson

ISBN-13: 978-0692824153
ISBN-10: 0692824154

DEDICATION

To You, Gentle Warrior, as you help to bring Peace and Light back into this world. This is for you.

CONTENTS

Meditation is the dissolution of thoughts in Eternal awareness or Pure consciousness without objectification, knowing without thinking, merging finitude in infinity.

Voltaire

INTRODUCTION

Welcome!

What I am going to share here is not likely going to be entirely new to you. However, the combination of your meditation practice with the power and energy of mandalas may enhance the way you experience life.

But first, what is a mandala? A mandala, Sanskrit for "circle", is a symbol representing the universe and wholeness. The meanings of individual mandalas are different and unique to each mandala. The goal of the mandala is to serve as a tool on your spiritual journey as it symbolizes order and as such, they make great tools for meditation and increasing self-awareness.

What about meditation? Meditation is a practice of mindful awareness. It describes a state of consciousness, where the mind is free of scattered thoughts. Whatever you do with awareness is meditation. That means it is more than just sitting in one spot with your eyes closed and trying to empty the mind. As long as you are being fully aware in the present moment, it is possible to meditate while walking or cooking as well as gazing at an image or simply focusing on the breath as you sit.

Meditation is a practice that gets easier with practice. Begin gently at first, maybe focusing on your breath for five seconds. Over time, those seconds add up to become minutes, and you can find yourself meditating for longer periods and while performing different activities.

The mandalas in *Pocket Mandalas* were especially created with the vibration and energy of a particular theme. Each is presented in combination with a few thoughts and a prayer to get you started on your meditation practice. You may even choose to create your own. Many of these prayers echo and are similar to each other – that is on purpose. A lot of these themes overlap to some extent, especially since the overall goal is to relieve stress in multiple areas of your life.

There is no particular order here. To use this book, simply set aside a few moments each day where you know you will not be disturbed and choose the theme or image that is drawing your attention most. Open yourself up to the energy if each theme, gaze on the image, and simply become aware of what feelings, thoughts, or ideas come up for you. As they come up, acknowledge them and let them pass. Your awareness will eventually focus solely on the image in front of you.

My hope is that as you spend time in meditation in the energy of these mandalas, your life becomes transformed into something more rich and fulfilling than you ever believed possible.

Best,
Melissa

FAMILY

Family can mean a lot of different things to different people. You may define it as consisting of your blood relatives, or you may feel that family for you is more the people you willingly choose to have in your life and share those aspects of you that you would not be able to share with anyone else. You may be very close to certain members of your family or you may find your relationships more strained than not.

Regardless of your personal definition of family, my wish is that you find the eternal love and support that you truly deserve from the people you care about and have in your life.

As I pray for my family, however I choose to define that for me, I open my heart to shine light upon each member of my family. And as that light is shone, I also open myself to receive the love and support they give me in return. Give us all the strength to overcome the difficulties that we are dealing with now, protect us against any and all problems we may encounter in the future, and help us all to remember that we are here for each other always.

In this moment now, I willingly choose to release any and all hurts that I may have experienced from my loved ones, and ask that they forgive me any hurts I have given them. May the love that binds us only grow stronger as we fulfill the destinies we have laid out before us.

2

MONEY

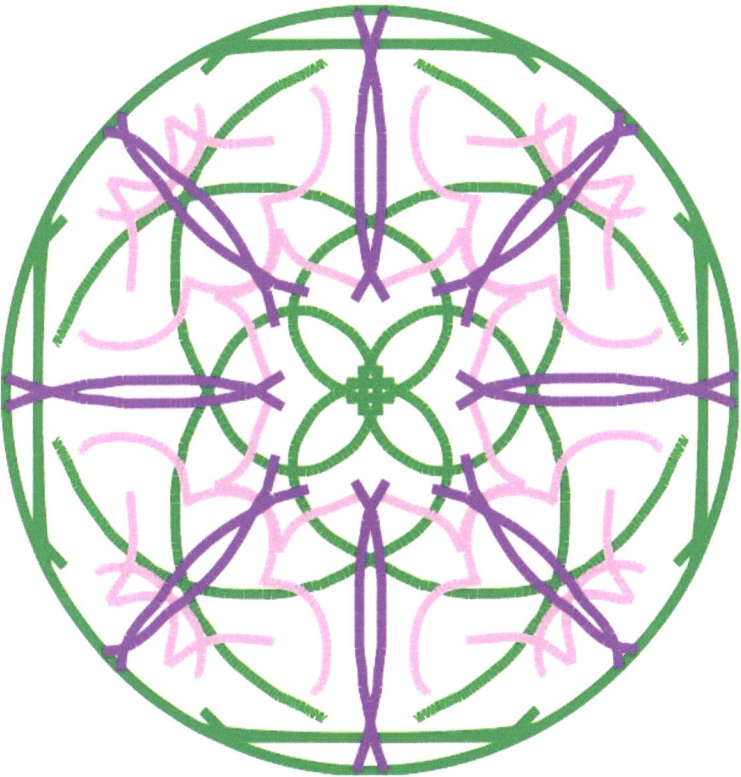

Money is a sensitive subject for many individuals, myself included. One thing to keep in mind though is that money itself is only a means of exchange. There is no good or bad money. You may perceive good or bad experiences as a result of certain transactions. You may have taken on certain stories as a result of what you have seen and witnessed in family members or other people in their dealings with money.

Whatever the history, know that in addressing your reactions to those situations and finding resolution, you begin to heal and change those stories surrounding money for you.

I know I complain about money a lot, and I know I worry about it too. However, I recognize that in reality, I am blessed and have all I need to survive and survive well. My financial struggles, as frustrating as they are, do not define me. They never have and they never will. I know I have the tools and the support I need to overcome my struggles with money, and I have access to the resources and power needed to create changes that will allow me to transform my financial situation.

I pray to open myself up to receive helpful guidance from my intuition and my guides. I allow them to help me shift and change my current money story into one where I am fully supported and cared for.

3

LETTING GO

There is such a strong desire to control what you can, as if you could make life behave exactly the way you want it. However, life has a funny way of constantly changing, and giving you challenges that you may or may not feel adequately prepared for. The beautiful and wonderful thing about life though is that no matter what happens, you *are* prepared and you *are* ready. You can choose to sit and wonder why things are happening the way they are, you can choose to complain, or, when you are ready, you can decide that staying stuck with a certain thought or situation is too much and it is time to move on.

Know that in letting go, you are not admitting defeat or weakness. Instead, you are realizing that your efforts are better spent elsewhere rather than trying to force something specific to happen.

I pray for the wisdom to know when to continue on and change the things I can and when to release and let go. I recognize that there are some things that I just cannot grasp or control, and I open myself up to realizing that surrendering for the time being is more than okay. If needed, I can always return to the situation at another point and address it with a clear head and clear heart.

I ask for my guides to help me during difficult times. Also, please make it easier for me to surrender as I transition towards letting go, with ever increasing faith and trust that all will be well.

4

LOVE

As the song goes, "love is a many splendored thing." Whether we are talking about romantic love, love for family members and friends, or love for self, you know there is always room for more love. Its very vibration is one of healing and growth so that while love itself may not be capable of physically tearing down brick walls, it is fully capable of softening hearts and leading to greater acceptance of self and others.

———————————————

As I sit and focus on my heart, I allow myself to feel extra love and gratitude toward being able to even experience and express love. I pray to hold on to this feeling each day, each moment, and bring love with me into each encounter.

I acknowledge that being this open with my heart may leave me feeling exposed or vulnerable to others. Help me to grow above that fear, to always feel safe in expressing and sharing love to myself and others, and to accept the vulnerability that comes from others expressing love to me in return.

5

INTIMACY

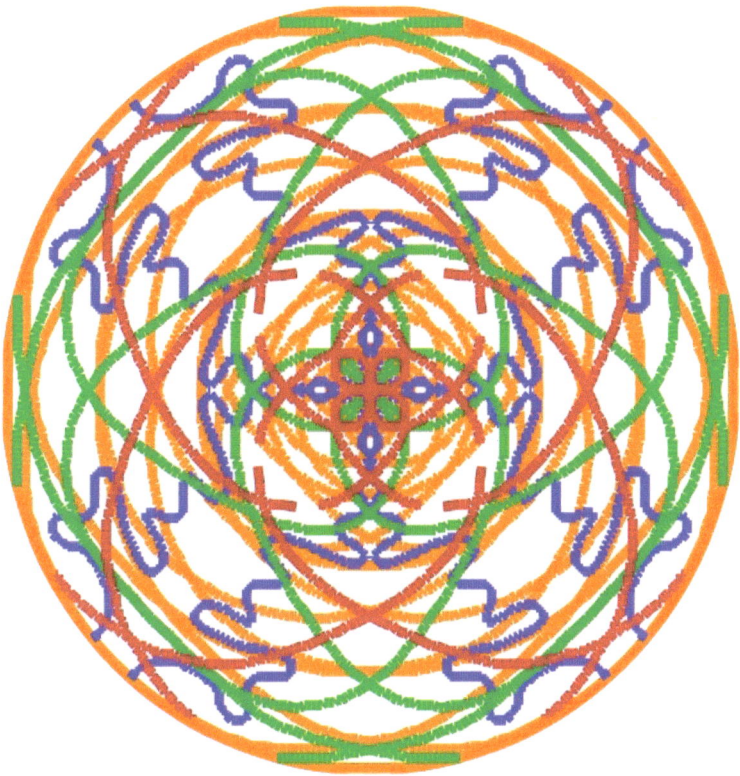

Being intimate with another person exposes yourself in a way that can make you seem especially vulnerable. You know you are sharing details about your life that you find important with someone else, and there may be a part of you that wonders if you are doing the right thing in placing trust in someone else to honor you and keep these details safe.

In the end, remember that we are all humans in want of a community to trust, and that it simply your choice as to how much you are willing to exchange and willing to give. And just as you open yourself up to being vulnerable, so they are to you.

I am scared. I am opening myself up to someone else, and I do not know if I can ever feel fully safe to share these pieces of me. However, despite my fear, I allow myself to dwell on the possibility that I am safe and that I will be better than okay.

Sharing these special parts of my world with others is a practice I can continue to build on, and I feel comfortable and supported, knowing I can go at the pace that is right and perfect for me.

6

CAREER

So let's get one thing straight – if you have a career, know that you are so much more than the title of your current occupation. And if you are looking for a career or looking to transition into something new, know that you are not limiting yourself by choosing one path or another that can provide for you.

As with anything else in life, things will continue to change. Keep an open heart and an open mind. Your work, paid or unpaid, adds value to the world though it may sometimes feel like it does not. Approach your work as one of many ways in which you contribute to those around you. And if you feel drawn to change focus, do so and know that nothing is ever fully out of reach.

I pray to always remember that the work I do, no matter how big or small it may seem, is always done with a good and kind heart, an open and inspired mind, and with diligence and enthusiasm. May this career fully support me and help me to always be able to provide for myself and to share with my loved ones.

WEIGHT AND THE PHYSICAL BODY

When was the last time you really, truly loved and accepted 100% of your body? Can you even remember a time when your physical appearance did not even matter?

Your body deserves a great deal more appreciation for all it does for you. Today, commit to building a healthy relationship with your body. Know that a lot of this begins with the willingness and the mindset to make better choices for yourself.

I only have this one body that takes care of me. It helps me to move around with relative ease. It does what it can from the foods and drinks I take in. Help me to please not be so critical and judgmental of my weight and body because it really does so much for me. I recognize that other people's perceptions of my physical appearance are their own and hold no influence on my own relationship with my body. What matters most here is that I open up to loving my body more and more because as I love it more, it will love me back.

Please give me the will I need to make the changes that my body needs. And while I realize my body is not going to change all at once, I do commit to being more mindful of how I treat it for the years to come.

8

MOTIVATION AND FOCUS

How often do you find yourself wishing that you had more time on your hands to accomplish everything that needs to get done? And then, rather than setting out to work on achieving those tasks, how often do you catch yourself going to check your email or social media instead just for a couple moments, only to look up at the clock and realize that an hour or more has flown by?

If you recognize this as all familiar to you, you can choose now as the perfect time to reset your mindset and reclaim your motivation and your focus.

In this moment, I willingly choose to connect to my power center, or Solar Plexus, as well as my creative center, or Sacral Chakra. In bringing my attention to these parts of my body, I tap into the piece of me that never falters, never goes out. Here, I am able to find both the inspiration as well as the energy to begin anew or continue moving forward toward an end-desire in mind.

I pray for the stamina to do what I must, to accomplish what I want, and to take care of myself in the meantime. I know my energy comes from the physical and mental support I give myself so I open myself up to allowing exactly that to occur, now and always.

9

HEALTH

There is more to your health than your physical condition and state. Remember that your mental, emotional, and spiritual states also contribute to your overall health and well-being.

It is when each of these areas are brought into balance that you can achieve "perfect" health, and that state is only going to be determined by you. There is no dictionary or doctor or societal definition that can truly encompass what is healthy for you. Look for the point where you feel at peace and ease with you and how you are.

I ask all parts of me to come together now – my emotions, my thoughts, my body, and my spirit. And with all parts of me here and present, I open myself up to the possibility of being truly and completely healthy and whole.

I ask that all parts of me work together to achieve that perfect and ideal balance for me. I am willing to put in the time and energy to make this happen, but I also open myself up to ask for the help and support from all sources to make it so.

10

BEING OPEN AND RECEIVING

Miracles abound and are always happening around you, but it takes an open mind and heart to appreciate those special moments as they come. And we are not even talking about big miracles like winning the lottery or landing the dream job, though those can certainly happen too.

For now, all I ask of you is to suspend judgment and criticism, bit by little bit over time. I invite you to stay in a state of wonder and curiosity. Doing so will help in opening yourself to witness the impossible actually become possible.

Dreaming seems so hard these days, especially when I feel like my dreams and wishes never come true. It feels like I am always being told that it is silly and foolish to ask for what I want and expect to actually receive them.

Yet, I know that miracles happen each and every day, each and every moment for other people. And if I know other people can experience miracles, then I know it can happen for me too. So with that in mind, I open my heart to the Universe and pray that my deepest desires and dreams and wishes be heard. I breathe with faith and trust that little by little, I can be open to these hopes and dreams coming into my life when they are in my best and highest interest, and I will receive these blessings with deep thanks and gratitude.

11

RELATIONSHIPS

Do you have any relationships that you wish were better at some level? Are they with loved ones? Are they with other people? Yourself? God or the Universe? What about your relationship with money? Your house? Your job? Do any of those want some of your attention as well?

In order to feel fully supported in life, it is important to continue nurturing and fostering those relationships that you want more support from. So if you want a better relationship with a loved one, put in the effort there with the faith that the effort will be reciprocated back to you somehow. If you want to get closer to God or your guides, begin the conversation there. For money, you can try to start by demanding less of it and seeing more of how it wants to support you and then taking the steps as you are guided to take them.

I know I keep coming back to the heart, but I also recognize that so much of my life is filtered through this part of me. As I breathe in and focus on my heart, I ask it to open and shine out on all the relationships I am holding in my mind this moment.

Help me to take the steps I need to foster and nurture this relationship so that I may continue to grow and learn. Help me to also be open to receiving the love and support I need and want in each of these relationships. I pray for balance and joy and more to be present in all of these partnerships.

12

JOY

Where is joy located on your priority list? If it is low, what can you do to bring it higher?

Having joy and experiencing it often helps to keep morale up. It also helps to generate motivation and drive to continue on as well as provides further inspiration to do, have, and be more in life and in general.

I invite you to make joy something you willingly incorporate more of into your life. Focus on what brings you happiness and let the rest go.

As I close my eyes, I call to attention now a time when I felt truly and completely happy. As I bask in this feeling of joy, I pray to have more experiences like this in all areas of my life.

Opening up to joy does not mean that I ignore or push aside other feelings like sadness, anger, or frustration. I promise to honor those emotions as they come up in time and feel through them. Right now though, I am making the choice to commit to live a life more in line with what makes my heart feel better and lighter, as I know this will help me accomplish so much more in life and help everyone around me do the same.

13

OVERCOMING FEAR

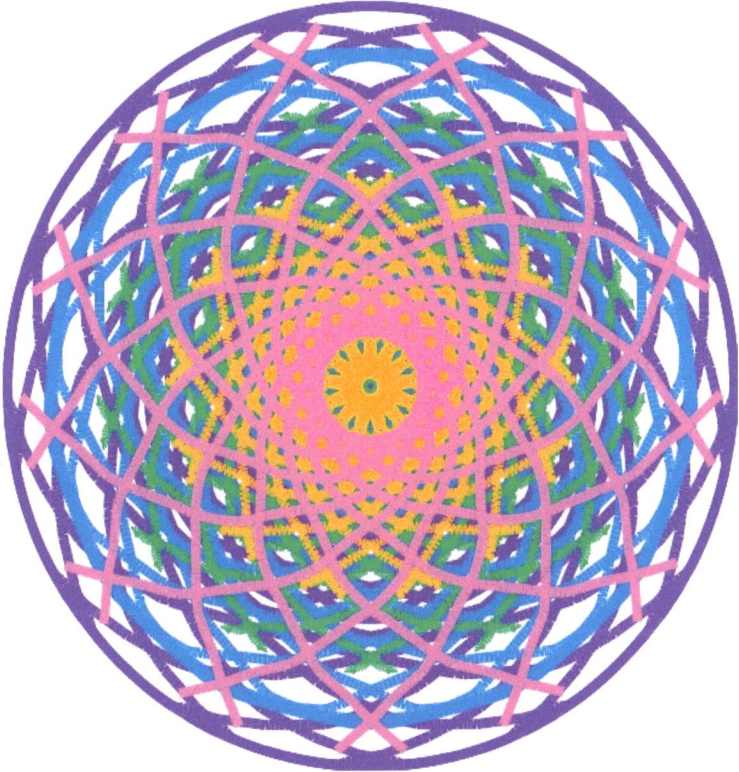

There is so much in this world to see, to witness, and to experience. However, fears of the unknown, fears around lack, fears around judgment, and so much more have a way of keeping you from dreaming of that big life much less experiencing everything life has to offer.

Whatever fears you have, known or unconsciously held onto, I invite you to accept the idea that perhaps these fears are holding you back needlessly. Take a look at the "what if's" that underlie many of your fears and be honest with yourself – is any of the stress or worry that you are feeding these fears worth the energy you are spending? If not, it may be time to let go.

I take these next few moments now to breathe into the center of my chest. There is such pressure here, a heavy weight that keeps me from breathing fully, and this pressure is coming from all the fears I hold about so many things. As I breathe, I slowly breathe out that pressure, that heaviness until I can breathe easy, knowing that in this moment, in this space, I am truly safe.

And once I reach that point where I can feel safe, I open myself up to the loving support of my guides, God, the Universe. I know that with that support, nothing can go wrong for me. I can choose to move through my days with more curiosity and excited anticipation rather than anxiety and worry, and I make that choice now. I choose now to continue bringing this feeling of being able to breathe deeply into all areas of my life, now and always.

14

JUDGMENT

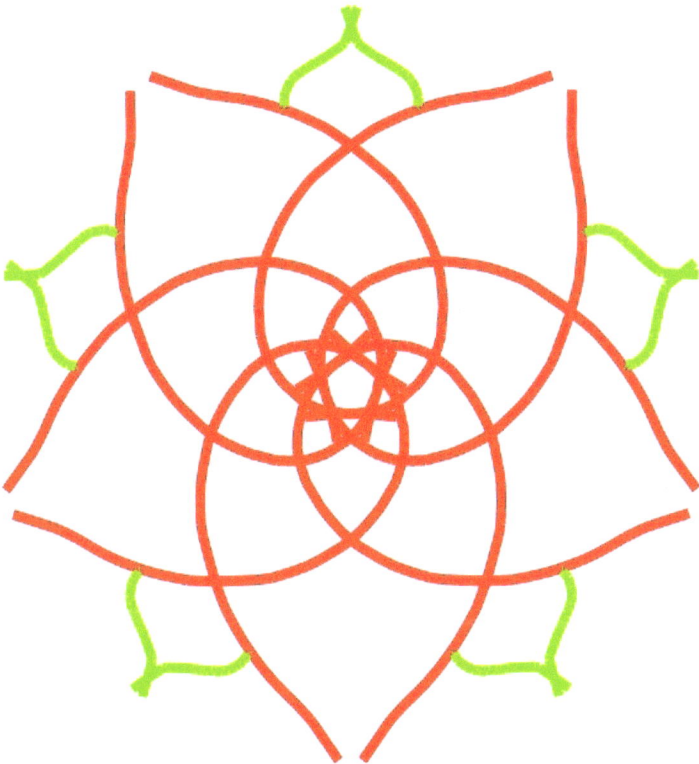

When a little child begins to learn how to crawl and walk, we praise him or her for each attempt rather than criticize that child with sharp words or actions for their failures. So at what point do we switch from love and support to making snap judgments toward others and ourselves? If it is to help you become better (at work, at home, as partners, etc.), do you feel like it has worked well for you, or do you feel like something else would be a better motivator?

I invite you now to break that pattern and habit of quick criticism. Such harsh words and actions will continue to wear you and your loved ones out. You may perceive it as tough love being able to push people for their best this way, but perhaps it is time to consider a different approach.

Who am I to judge others when I know I am nowhere near perfect myself? Instead, I give myself permission now to release that judgment and anything connected to being so critical. I suspend the limitations that get implemented when these are in place and release them.

In this moment, I commit to being gentle and loving toward myself and others instead, and cultivating a more peaceful and loving environment within me and outside of me.

15

FOOD

There are many excuses to continue making the food choices we currently make. Some foods bring comfort. Some foods are easier to prepare or are more convenient than others. Money can sometimes influence the foods you decide to purchase too.

Whatever those excuses are, know that you do not have to hang onto those stories. Now is the perfect time to begin cultivating a healthy relationship between you and your body. Remember that what you put into it, what you feed it (and that s more than just nutritional food) will help shape and determine how you live in the future. So choose wisely, starting here, starting now.

———————————

I know my mind, body, and soul requires good food and nutrition to function as optimally as possible. At this moment, I choose to make a more conscious effort to listen to my body. That includes only taking in what is truly beneficial for me and my well-being and also listening to when my body wants to be fed.

I pray to let go of the cravings, the poor habits, and the excuses I have for not making myself more of a priority. What has been done in the past need no longer apply now, and I step forward toward a better, healthier me.

16

PHYSICAL ACTIVITY

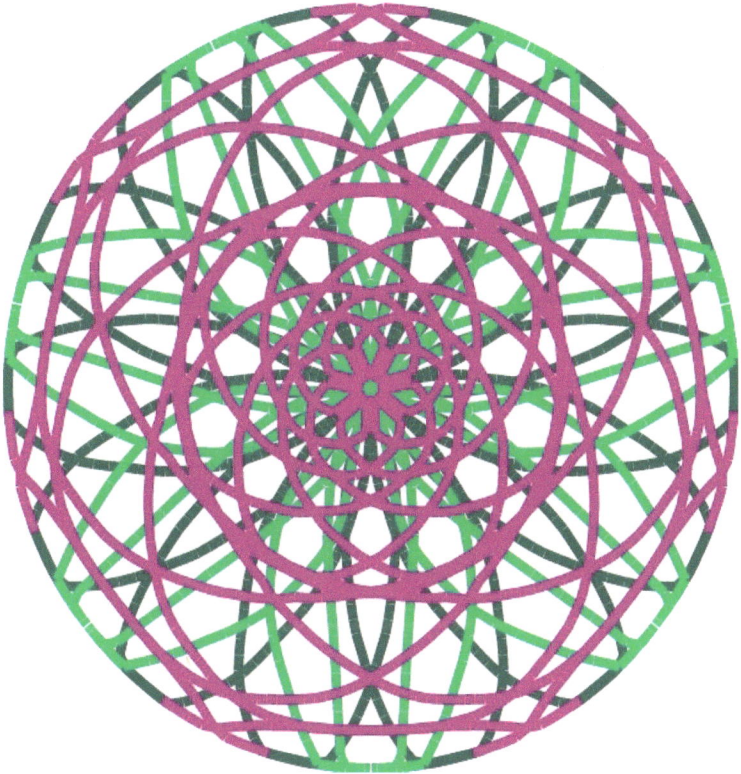

It is no secret. Ours is a society where the norm and goal even is to live a sedentary lifestyle. Yet you are likely being bombarded by your doctors, by the news and media, and by society in general about the importance of physical activity. So what will it take for you to choose the active route?

Your body needs you to stay engaged, and physical activity is actually one of the best ways to stay grounded and centered when all else seems to be getting out of hand. It is time for you to listen to your body – its wisdom will guide you into doing what you need to do.

It is time. My body needs me to treat it better, and I make that commitment here and now to follow through on that. I vow to do what it takes to move my body in a way to help it become fit, toned, and strong. I know that does not mean jumping straight into a rigorous exercise routine that will wear me out and discourage me from further exercise. Instead, I will ease into a routine with guidance and direction from my body, my health care providers, and my guides as needed.

The more I do now, I know I will be rewarded with less pain and aches in the future. I pray for the strength and endurance to stick with this commitment that I have made with myself.

17

CONFIDENCE

Dwelling in the space of "what if" uses up much of your time and energy. Fear of the unknown and resistance to change can stunt growth and the ability to capitalize on opportunities as they present themselves to you. Criticism and opposition from others can lead to second guessing the value of your own thoughts, ideas, and beliefs.

Now, more than ever before though, you are being called to be the truest, most authentic you possible. In all areas of our life, that means taking the extra step of really figuring out what your values are and then standing by your words and actions when they resonate with your truth. The courage to do so can be found inside of you, though know that you can also rely on your external support team too. Trust and know that you are valuable, you have worth.

There are times when life becomes difficult, when the choices I need to make seem so big, or when I am faced with potential opposition or criticism from others that I know I need to ask for help. In times as these, help me to remember to breathe and connect to my power center, my Solar Plexus. Here, I know I can find the confidence and power that is always available within me and tap into it anytime I need. I breathe deeply now, and feel that light growing and expanding throughout me.

I stand firm in me and myself.

18

COMPASSION

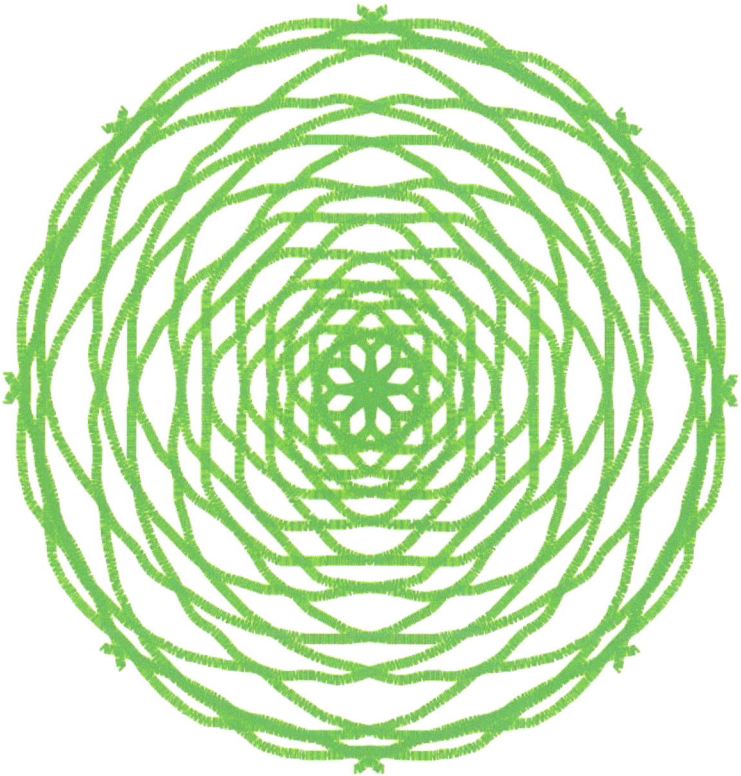

Remember, you are no better or worse than your fellow human being. Instead, the situations and path you face may differ and may be one of more or less privilege. The challenges placed in front of you do not negate or belittle another individual's trials.

In light of this, be mindful to overlook any sense of superiority that may come up and treat one and all with the same, generous love and respect as you would a loved one.

———

I pray to help remember that the journey other people are on are their own. Let me not be so quick to judge and criticize as I can never truly know the full extent of what someone else is going through. Rather, during those periods of difficulty, I pray to show and demonstrate compassion, caring, and comfort instead.

In sharing of my heart in this way with others, I open myself to receiving more compassion in return. I hold space that such exchange provides the healing and support we all need.

19

HOPE

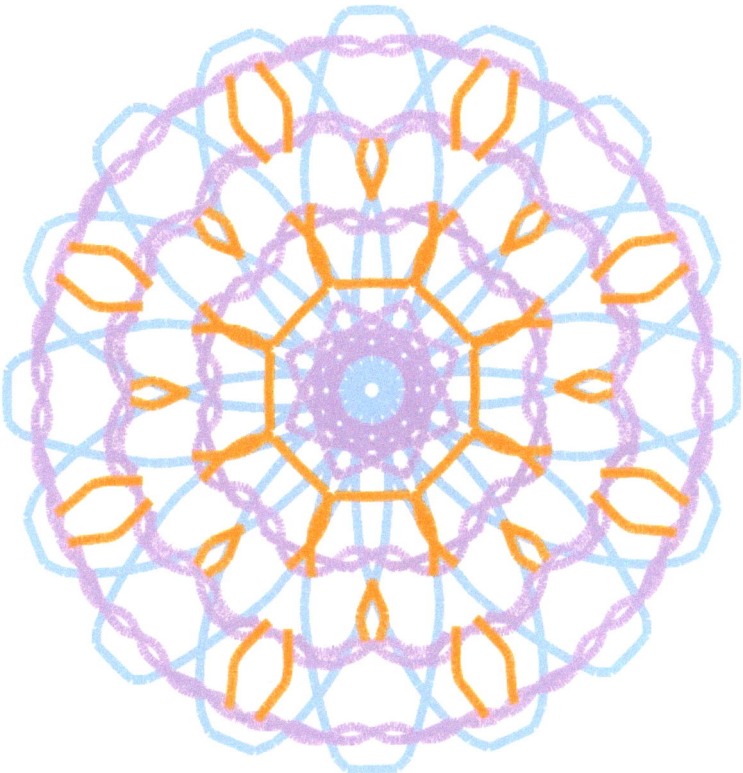

When all light seems to be gone from the world, you may find yourself looking deep within and without to find the things that continue to bring light and joy in life. In times such as these, it is helpful to keep a sort of list handy to remind you of the things you have to look forward to, people, places, or projects to turn to when life gets difficult and overwhelming.

To have hope means to remember that a new day will always come, the sun will always return, that good will always follow bad, and that life will continue. Choose to ride the waves of whatever life is giving you, and know that in light of everything you face, this too shall pass.

In times of confusion, stress, and worry, I pray to always look for the light, to hang onto faith, and to trust that all will be well in the end. I know that this hope I hold for me and for others helps to keep us moving forward, even when all else seems to be going and turning against us.

I visualize this hope as a gentle pink light radiating out from my heart and growing so it encompasses me. As I move about my days with this pink light, I help to spread hope to the world around me.

20

FAITH AND SPIRITUALITY

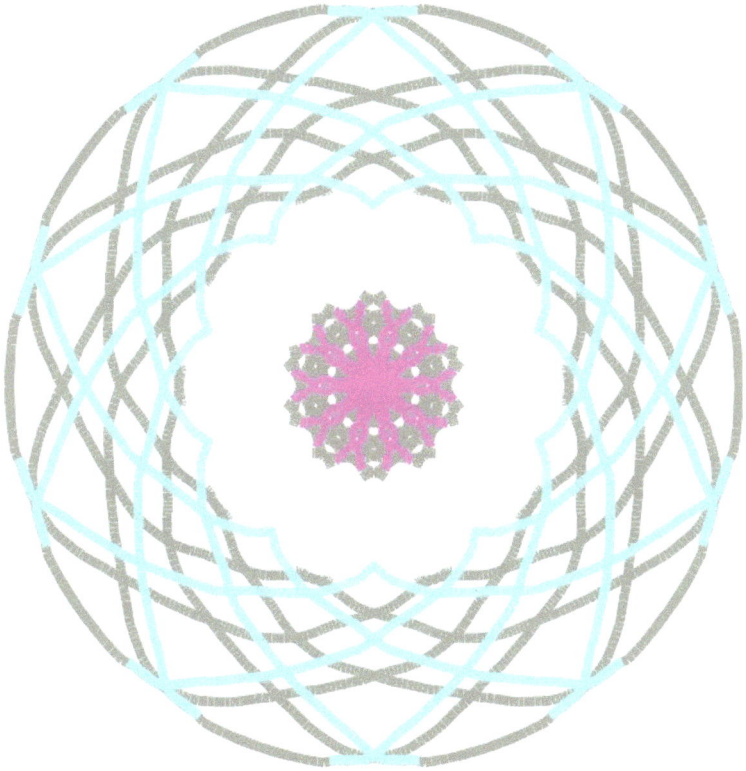

Whether or not you believe in God or another higher power, cultivate the idea and the ability of having faith in something bigger than yourself. Doing so can help put your efforts and trials in perspective when looked at from the bigger picture.

From that vantage point, you matter, much more than you can ever realize. Your very presence, in combination with everything you do, creates ripple effects that help change the world. Have faith and maintain a sense of spirituality to help nurture your soul self at a level that can bring you more peace and general ease.

I pray to open myself up to the possibility of believing in something that I cannot perceive, that I cannot understand, that I cannot prove to really exist. Yet, deep in my heart, I know there is something there, always in the background, creating and orchestrating the miracles in my life and overseeing the path that I take as it intertwines with those around and beyond me.

If there are angels, spirits, God – please help me to believe, in spite of my doubts and disbeliefs.

21

SELF CARE

Are you going through your days in a mental and physical fog? Where you try to please everyone and get everything done and leave yourself so worn out at the end of the day that you cannot even sleep because your mind keeps racing about everything that needs to happen tomorrow or the day after?

It is time to change that and get back to taking care of you. It is going to take a good conscious effort on your part to incorporate more loving and caring for yourself in order to break the destructive habits you have created for yourself thus far. Still, recognize that in taking care of yourself, you will be better able to take care of everything else going on around you.

———————————

I acknowledge the fact that I have not been the gentlest or most loving of caretakers to myself. But I call all of me into the present moment to bear witness to my desire for change. I know that in the end, the best person to take care of me is me, and to that end, I vow to take one or more extra steps to show myself kindness and love, each and every day.

In being able to take care of myself, I know I will be better prepared to not only accomplish everything that needs to be done but also take actual steps toward achieving those goals and dreams I keep putting off. I pray for the guidance to always know how to best take care of myself in each moment so that I am free from the weariness that drains me currently.

22

PHILANTHROPY

You and I, we are not on this planet all alone, isolated in our respective bubbles, though at times it may feel that way. Remember, anything and everything you do has an impact on others around you. Be mindful and try to make those thoughts, words, and actions be only those of the highest light and good for all.

Your work can add to the work of those around you. From that space of knowledge, know that we can truly transform the world into one of peace and love.

I recognize that I live a very blessed life, and for this, I am ever grateful. From my plenty, I know I can give much to my family, my neighbor, my colleague, the stranger, and the world. Help give me the courage and faith needed to spread and share in those blessings with those who are in need of such light in their own lives.

Help me and help us come together to make the world a better place for all who dwell here.

23

CULTURE

Who you are is a culmination of all facets of your past – how you were brought up, the ideas passed onto you from your parents or caregivers, the places you lived in, the societal ideas that you grew up with and took on over time, and so much more. That rich history that you bring with you make up a truly wonderful and unique you, a you that brings so much light to this world.

Remember that you are not limited by the definition of that culture. Your identity cannot be defined by one part alone. So honor that richness. Honor that culture that helps to define you.

My identity is tied to my history, which itself has its roots and foundations in the very way I was brought up and raised. Living as I do now, I give credit and thanks for my background as it has helped me to be the best person I am today.

I pray that I continue to honor and show respect to my past so that I can show honor and respect to those of the future, by embodying and embracing the best of my beliefs, heritage, and culture.

24

SOVEREIGNTY

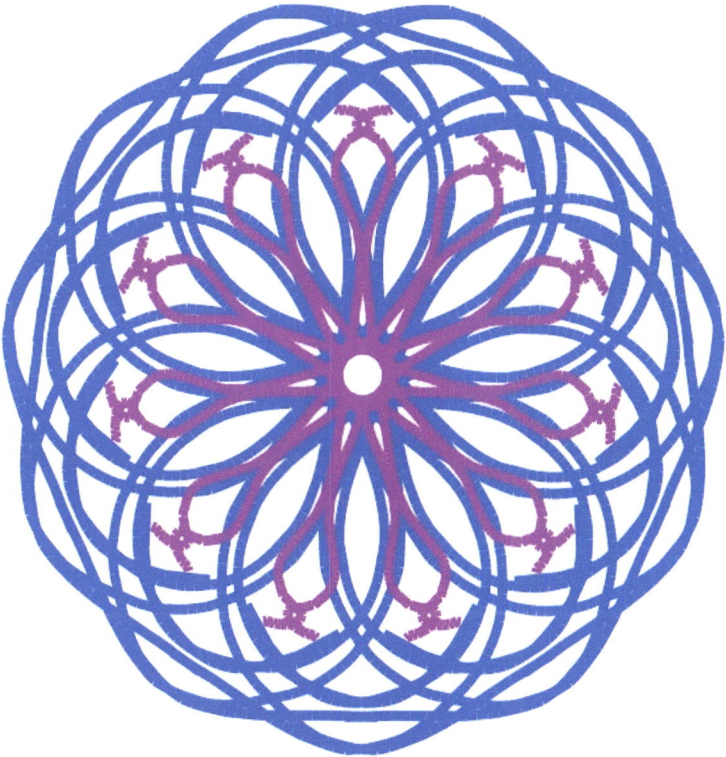

Do you have a good sense of who you are at the core level? What you stand for and what you believe to be true? How do you feel when you are asked to stand by your thoughts, ideas, and beliefs? Are you confident and clear when expressing yourself to others? Or do you find yourself backing off when faced with personalities who challenge you and believe their way is the only way?

Remember that you are every bit as worthy and deserving as anyone else. I bear witness to the grandness that is you and the good heart and spirit that drive you. Feel that resonate within you and step forward with the inherent power and grace that is all your own.

I matter. My thoughts and opinions matter. I choose to carry myself with the same grace, ease, and confidence as any noble and kind hearted royal of the past as they watched over their respective domains.

I recognize that I am here not to dictate or lord over others, but to learn from others and guide by deed and example. From this moment onward, I will not allow my words and actions to be lost or misunderstood, though I realize there will be times that necessitate compromise. I pray that by standing in my sovereignty, that I can be an example to those who look to me for help and support.

25

ENERGY

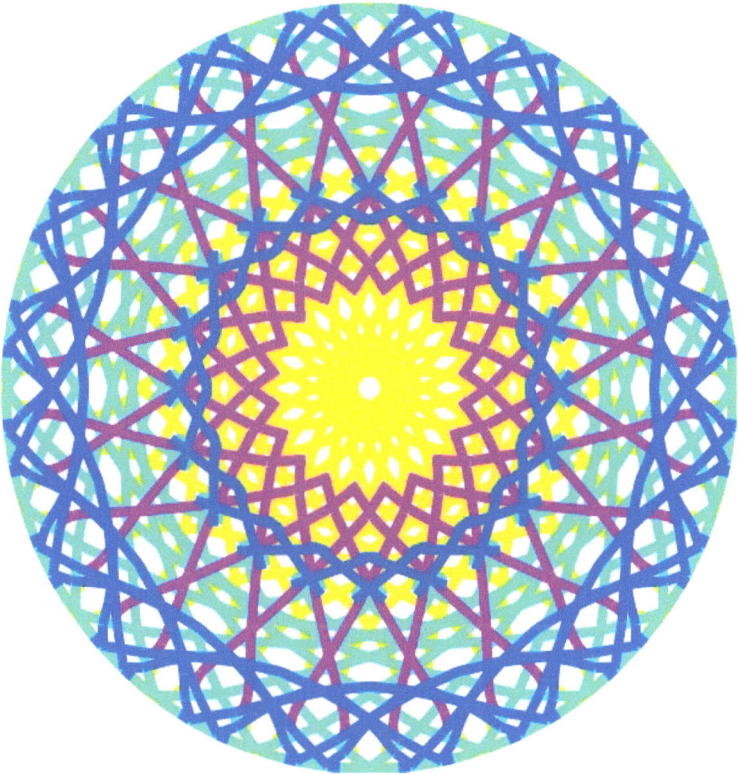

How often do you find yourself wishing for more energy during the day? Do you feel like your to-do list continues to grow and that in the end, nothing significant seems to get done? Now what if, instead, it is not the energy that is lacking but the inability to use the energy you do have more efficiently?

The opportunity here for you is to be mindful and take care of yourself. Honor the boundaries that you set so others cannot take advantage of the time and energy that is meant to take care of you and your needs. You have the potential to do so much more, but it takes getting to know your own abilities and limitations first and respecting that.

I ask now for the ability to rest soundly each night and awaken each morning refreshed and renewed, with more than enough energy to carry me through the day. Help me to keep my focus and drive to accomplish what I can.

And on those days when I find myself running low on drive and motivation, let me find the support and help I need from those around me, from my guides, from God, and the Universe. I know nothing is placed in front of me that I cannot handle, but I also admit that I cannot do everything on my own. Help me to remember that this is not a sign of weakness or failure on my part to ask for help as I need.

26

BEING DILIGENT AND ENTHUSIASTIC

Not everything you do will be exciting or inspiring. Yet oftentimes, those things need to be done in order to get to the next step or to achieve the next goal.

When you are lost in the monotony or drudgery of a task, it may be useful to step back for a few moments and see the work as part of an overall bigger picture. When you are reminded about the reason behind each task, you may find the inspiration and drive to keep going. Remember to try and bring joy and curiosity to each project and you will find yourself moving through the mundane more quickly.

Too often, I go through my life in a daze, caught up in a routine that, while predictable and easy, does not fully engage me in mind, body, or spirit. In acknowledging that, I consciously begin to open myself up to viewing these tasks and working on them with a freshness and curiosity that has been lacking up to now. And when it feels like there is no end in sight, let me find the diligence and enthusiasm I need to continue on until I am able to reach the end goal.

Help me to bring this perspective into all that I do so that I may not grow bored or weary. And I set the intention that all my actions engage me and leave me feeling fulfilled and accomplished.

27

HOME AND SPACE

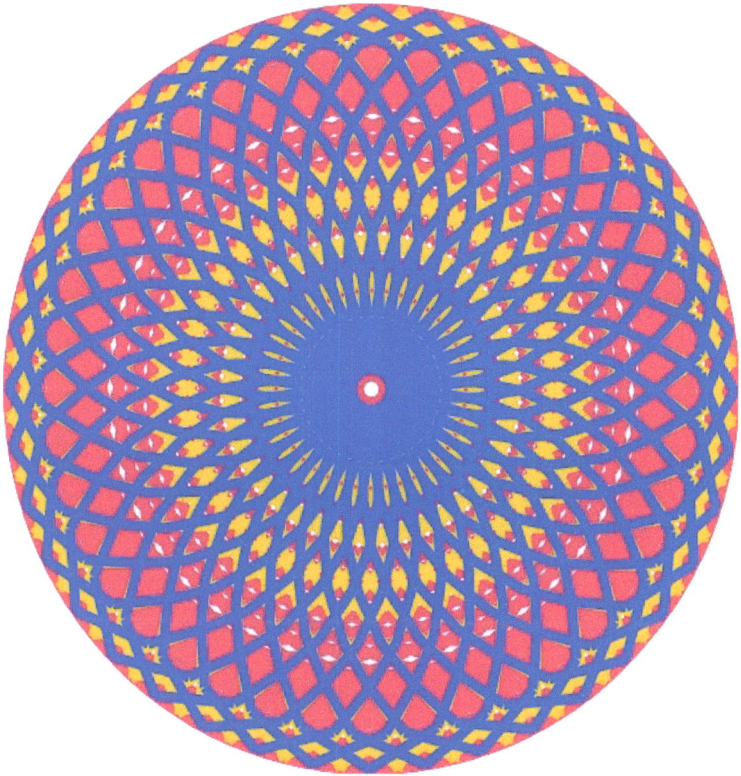

Your environment is a physical extension of yourself. So with that in mind, how would you describe your space? Do you find your living conditions warm and inviting? Cluttered and cramped? Light and airy or dark and dreary? Do you enjoy where you live now or do you find yourself wanting to move?

Just as it is important to take care of your physical body, it is also important to honor the spaces where you spend much of your time, be it home, work, in transit, or elsewhere. Consciously make the effort to take care of the space around you, change it if you need, and release the items that no longer bring you joy.

Knowing that what is inside of me is mirrored externally, I make the commitment here and now that as I continue to change and shift and grow into a better person that my external environment changes and shifts and transforms to match the energy I wish to project.

Finding that balance is important. As I take care of my home, I know it will help me to feel safe, grounded, and supported.

28

ADDICTIONS AND HABITS

Why do you choose to do what you do, especially when you know certain actions are not for your highest and best good? Can you readily and easily admit to yourself that there are certain patterns or routines that may be causing you or your loved ones heartache and grief?

Stepping into admission of an addiction or harmful habit is difficult, but it is the first step to getting support. Know that you are never alone in your journey and that help is readily available should you seek it and ask. There is absolutely nothing you cannot overcome, as painful or as troublesome as it may seem.

This addiction, this habit – I recognize now that it is a way to keep me hiding, to keep me being small and not standing fully in my truly perfect and authentic self. I know I am greater than this and can offer so much more if I just release these patterns.

I may have tried to do so in the past, a number of times actually, and each time has been met with failure. I commit now to not fail. And I ask those who support me to do so now during this difficult period. It may not be easy and I may feel like I am moving backwards rather than forward as I try to change, but I will hold onto the faith I need to push through this and come out the other side with success.

29

GRATITUDE

Can you make thanksgiving more than a holiday you observe once a year? Giving thanks and living a life of gratitude lightens both head and heart as you delve into the magnitude of how blessed and lucky you are to be alive here this day, this moment. You may be surrounded by people who love you and care for you, or have work to look forward to, or have shelter and a roof over your head, or can wake up each day knowing that you have more time yet ahead of you to do something great.

All of these blessings are not afforded to just anyone, so take the time to give thanks now and give thanks often.

———————————————

As I look here at all the riches I have surrounded myself with, I take the moment now to sit back and bask and marvel at how blessed I am. I become aware of a feeling of gratitude that builds and grows, bubbling up from the middle of my chest until it feels like it will burst and overflow with the feeling. I let it.

And in doing so, I radiate out love and light to all the world around me, blessing the world as it has blessed me.

30

PEACE

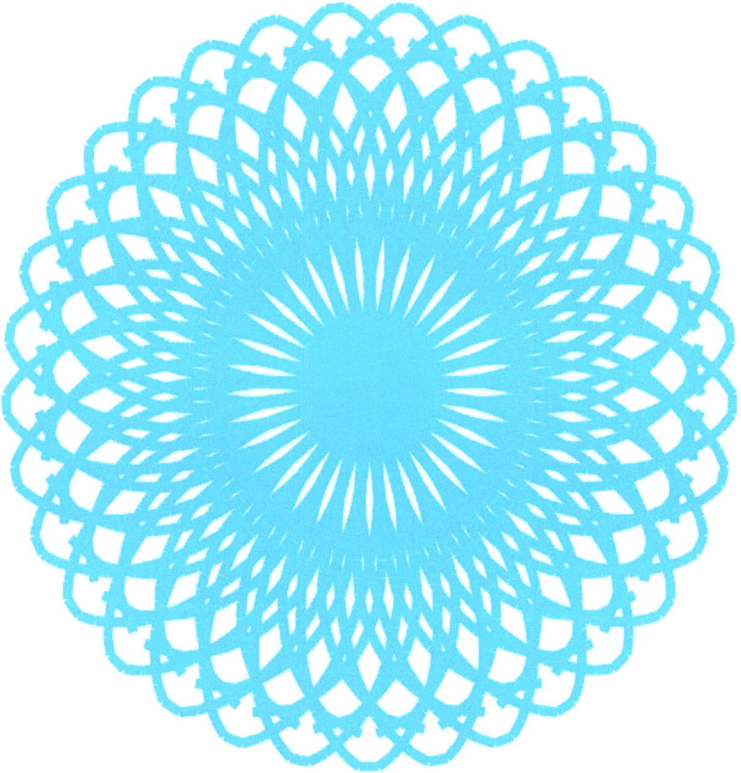

One of my deepest wishes for you is that you experience peace. As I hold space for you through this journey, I pray that you shift and grow and transform and change in a way that makes you even more the spectacular you that you are.

May the feelings of joy and ease permeate you throughout the day as you begin to embrace and live the notion that all is well.

I invoke peace here in this moment. I ask myself to embody and embrace that peace, now and always. Let that peace be cultivated and spread, from my thoughts, my words, and my actions.

May that peace be shared and gifted to each and every individual I come across today and always. Let the peace that begins with me ripple out and spread, leading to healing of the world at large. I hold the intent that this is so, and so it is.

WHAT'S NEXT?

Now that you have gone through this visual meditation journey and gained some peace and healing for yourself, you might be wondering what is next for you.

If you would like a guide seeing how you can use crystals in your meditation practice, I invite you to check out my book, *Your Crystal Journey:*

http://www.amazon.com/dp/B01DJDN54W

If you would like a guide specifically for effectively maintaining a healthy work-life balance by managing stress, my book, *Remembering to Breathe*, may assist you:

http://www.amazon.com/dp/B00UGIBAIM

You can also connect with me directly on my website. I often post questions and exercises that challenge you to integrate mind, body, and spirit there, as well as offer a variety of services and other goods to energetically assist you. Sign up for the newsletter to receive a powerful guided meditation where you can meet your higher self and never miss out on the latest news:

http://melissavaldellon.com/

Lastly, I want to express my sincerest thanks to you for taking your time to read through this entire guide and making the commitment to cultivating inner peace. I hope you enjoyed these meditations and found them useful towards your healing.

If you found this book helpful and liked it, I would greatly appreciate it if you took a moment to leave a review on Amazon and share this guide with others via social media:

http://www.amazon.com/dp/B01MT28WM3

ABOUT THE AUTHOR

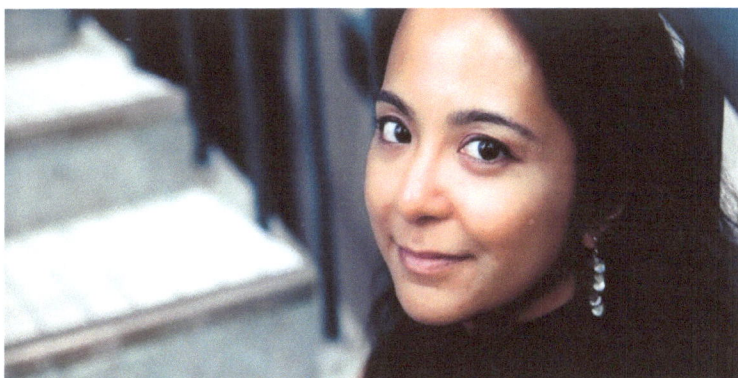

MELISSA VALDELLON has made it her mission in this lifetime to light your inner flame and inspire you to share and spread that light far and wide.

Melissa has spent this and many lifetimes as a teacher, traditional/native practitioner, healer, priest/priestess, warrior, protector, and more. She draws from a rich depth of experience as she continues to re-awaken to divine knowledge, with the help of her angelic and spiritual team. She knows what it's like to spend years suppressing and denying her given gifts and talents, and ever since she emerged from the spiritual closet, she is passionate about helping others to do the same.

While she currently spends much of her time as an optometrist seeing patients and teaching at the UC Berkeley School of Optometry, she also dedicates much of her time to self-care by meditating, reading, listening to music, spending time with her furry loved ones, visiting the beach, and writing. With three books already published and at least three more on the way, Melissa is certainly keeping busy, but not too busy as to be unavailable to you. You can contact her by email directly on her website, http://melissavaldellon.com/, and she will personally get back to you shortly.

www.ingramcontent.com/pod-product-compliance
Lightning Source LLC
Chambersburg PA
CBHW051235090426
42740CB00001B/30